Wonders of the Sea

Coral Reefs

Kimberley Jane Pryor

Smart Apple Media

Smart Apple Media
2140 Howard Drive West
North Mankato, Minnesota 56003

First published in 2007 by
MACMILLAN EDUCATION AUSTRALIA PTY LTD
627 Chapel Street, South Yarra, Australia 3141

Visit our Web site at www.macmillan.com.au or go directly to www.macmillanlibrary.com.au

Associated companies and representatives throughout the world.

Library of Congress Cataloging-in-Publication Data

Pryor, Kimberley Jane.
    Coral reefs / by Kimberley Jane Pryor.
    p. cm. — (Wonders of the sea)
    Includes index.
    ISBN 978-1-59920-140-5
    1. Coral reef ecology—Juvenile literature. I. Title.

    QH541.5.C7P79 2007
    577.7'89—dc22

6386

2007004882

Edited by Erin Richards
Text and cover design by Christine Deering
Page layout by Domenic Lauricella
Photo research by Legend Images

Printed in U.S.

Acknowledgements
The author and the publisher are grateful to the following for permission to reproduce copyright material:

Cover photograph: Coral reef courtesy of Digital Vision.

age fotostock/Georgie Holland, p. 27 (right); Karen Gowlett-Holmes/AUSCAPE, p. 26; Doug Perrine/AUSCAPE, p. 18; Coo-ee Picture Library, pp. 15, 19; Digital Vision, pp. 1, 7, 12 (top), 23; Dreamstime, pp. 3, 5, 11, 13 (bottom), 14, 16, 17, 25, 28, 30; Eva Boogaard/Lochman Transparencies, p. 9; Clay Bryce/Lochman Transparencies, p. 29; Chris Surman/Lochman Transparencies, p. 13 (top); Lonely Planet Images/Robert Halstead, p. 20; Lonely Planet Images/Laura Losito, p. 27 (left); Lonely Planet Images/Casey & Astrid Witte Mahaney, p. 21; Lonely Planet Images/Leonard Douglas Zell, p. 12 (bottom); NASA Goddard Space Flight Center, p. 4; Photolibrary.com/OSF/David B. Fleetham, p. 22; Photolibrary.com/OSF/Paul Kay, p. 24; Photolibrary.com/Pacific Stock/Jim Watt, p. 10; Photolibrary.com/Photo Researchers Inc, p. 8; Photolibrary.com/Matthew Oldfield, Scubazoo/Science Photo Library, p. 6.

While every care has been taken to trace and acknowledge copyright, the publisher tenders their apologies for any accidental infringement where copyright has proved untraceable. Where the attempt has been unsuccessful, the publisher welcomes information that would redress the situation.

For Nick, Thomas and Ashley
– Kimberley Jane Pryor

Contents

Glossary words
When a word is printed in **bold**, you can look up its meaning in the glossary on page 31.

The sea

The sea is a very large area of salty water.
It covers most of Earth's surface.

The blue part of Earth is the sea.

The sea has many different **habitats**. Coral reefs are habitats that are found in warm, shallow water.

Some coral reefs lie in shallow water around islands.

Coral reefs

Coral reefs are areas covered with corals. Corals are groups of small animals called coral polyps.

Corals come in many shapes and colors.

Coral reefs are full of life. They provide food and shelter for many different plants and animals.

Colorful fish live on coral reefs.

Plants

Tiny plants, called algae, grow inside most corals. They make food and **oxygen** for the corals. The tiny plants also give the corals their different colors.

The green colors on the coral polyps are tiny plants.

Larger plants, called seaweed, grow on coral reefs.
They are food for sea urchins and plant-eating fish.

Green seaweed
sometimes grows
near corals.

Animals

Many different animals live on coral reefs. In the daytime, fish feed among the corals. Shrimps wander over sea urchins, and sea cucumbers crawl along the sand.

Coleman shrimps are often found on sea urchins.

As the sun sets, daytime feeders hide under the corals. Night-time feeders swarm out and start hunting for food.

Blue-spotted stingrays hunt for food at night.

Where animals live

On a coral reef, each kind of animal has a special place to live.

Moon jellyfish float near the surface of the water.

Giant clams sit on the sea floor.

Sooty terns fly
above the reef
looking for food.

Emperor angelfish swim
around the corals.

Survival

To survive on a coral reef, animals need to find and eat food. A coral polyp uses stinging tentacles to **paralyze** tiny animals that float by.

A coral polyp draws food to its mouth with its tentacles.

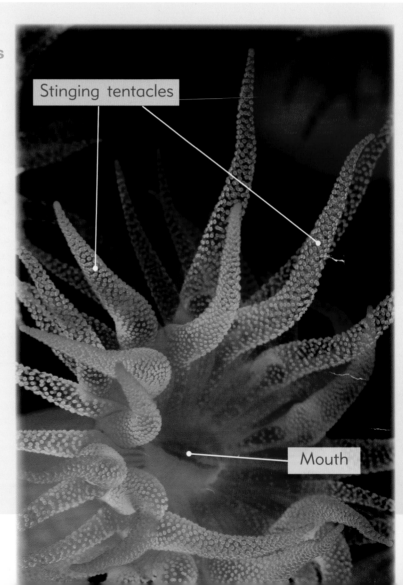

Stinging tentacles

Mouth

Animals also need to protect themselves from **predators**. Some use their colors, and others use their body parts.

Flat body for hiding between corals

Black patch to hide eyes from predators

False eye to trick predators

Long-nosed butterfly fish use their shape and pattern to help them avoid predators.

Small animals

Small animals live all over coral reefs. In the daytime, crabs scurry across the sand. Sea slugs slide over corals and sometimes over sea squirts.

Some sea slugs are very colorful.

Feather stars feed at night. They stretch out their arms to catch tiny floating animals to eat.

Feather stars often climb to the top of a coral reef to catch food.

Large animals

Large animals find plenty of food on coral reefs. Turtles eat seaweed that grows on corals. They also eat some animals that live on coral reefs.

Loggerhead sea turtles eat small animals, such as lobsters.

Dolphins usually hunt in groups, called pods.
They help each other find and catch squids
and fish to eat.

Bottlenose dolphins sometimes hunt on coral reefs.

Fish

Fish that live on coral reefs are often brightly colored.

Squarespot anthias are very colorful coral reef fish.

Bright colors help a fish to find others of the same kind. They also help a fish to find a **mate**.

Masked butterfly fish keep the same mate for life.

Along with bright colors, some fish have spots and others have stripes. These patterns help them blend in with the corals.

The stripes on moorish idols help confuse predators.

Sharks are large fish that hunt for food at night. Their sense of smell helps them find fish hiding under corals.

Whitetip reef sharks have a very good sense of smell.

Living together

Sometimes animals live together for protection. Some fish swim in a group, called a school. This makes it harder for a predator to choose and catch a fish.

The red lionfish is hunting a school of glassfish.

Some animals survive by living with another kind of animal. Clownfish live in sea anemones. The stinging tentacles of the sea anemone protect the clownfish from predators.

The sea anemone protects the clownfish that lives in it.

Food chain

Living things depend on other living things for food. This is called a food chain.

This is how a food chain works.

Plant

food for

This is a simple coral reef food chain.

food for

Seaweed makes food using energy from the sun.

Plant-eating animal  food for **Animal-eating animal**

  food for

Seaweed is food for blue tangs.

Blue tangs are food for tiger groupers.

Threats to coral reefs

Coral reefs can be **threatened** by natural events, such as storms. Big waves can damage coral reefs. The crown-of-thorns starfish is also a threat because it eats corals.

Crown-of-thorns starfish can harm coral reefs.

Coral reefs are also threatened by people who:

- put garbage into the sea
- catch so many fish that some are in danger of becoming **extinct**
- drag boat anchors and fishing nets across corals
- touch or walk on corals

Fishing nets can damage coral reefs.

Protecting coral reefs

We help protect coral reefs when we:

- put garbage into garbage cans
- stop catching **threatened fish**
- tie our boats to **buoys**
- look at corals but do not touch them

Divers enjoy looking at plants and animals on coral reefs.

Glossary

buoys floating balls, tied by chain to concrete blocks on the sea floor

extinct no longer existing

habitats places where plants or animals naturally grow or live

mate one of a pair of animals, a male and a female

oxygen the gas in air and water that animals need to breathe to stay alive

paralyze to make something unable to move

predators animals that hunt, kill, and eat other animals

threatened placed in danger

threatened fish fish that are in danger of becoming extinct

Index